Brenda and the Bird

A Division of The **McGraw·Hill** Companies

Columbus, Ohio

www.sra4kids.com

SRA/McGraw-Hill

A Division of The **McGraw·Hill** *Companies*

Printed in the United States of America.

Send all inquiries to:
SRA/McGraw-Hill
8787 Orion Place
Columbus, OH 43240-4027

ISBN 0-07-569484-0
  2 3 4 5 6 7 8 9 DBH 05 04 03 02

Brenda has a bird on her shirt.

Brenda sees a bird just like the bird
on her shirt!

At first Brenda just watches the bird.

The bird gets a dirt bath.

Brenda gets a dirt bath, too!

Mom is firm. "Brenda, you are a girl, not a bird! Now you must have a water bath."